TRANSITION

From Widowhood...

...To Womanhood

MINISTER MARY D. EDWARDS

PUBLISHED by
LEAVES OF GOLD CONSULTING, LLC
P.O. Box 21818 - Detroit, MI 48221
LeavesofGoldConsulting.com
leavesofgold.llc@gmail.com

ISBN: 0-9710482-5-8

Printed in the United States of America

For more information, contact:
Minister Mary D. Edwards
Leaves of Gold Consulting, LLC
LeavesofGoldConsulting.com
Leavesofgold.llc@gmail.com

Book cover and page design by
Shannon Crowley for Treasure Image & Publishing
TreasureImagePublishing.com

Dedication and Appreciation

To the churches, businesses, individuals, and organizations that have shown concern for widows according to James 1:27, thank you. Thank you for your prayers, volunteer services, financial support, and guidance. A special thank you to the Detroit Area Agency on Aging. They offered me an opportunity to write and narrate 15 two-minute tips for widows on their regular Saturday morning radio program. The Bible says that we should not despise the day of small beginnings (Zech. 4:10). As a result, this handbook was conceived and further developed. There is also a companion audio available without the awesome testimonies of the nine widows in this book.

To the widows who so graciously shared their hearts with us and offer encouragement.

His Lovely Wife Ministries and Widows With Wisdom thank Mr. Gasper Gammachia for helping to make the production of this book possible.

To my late husband, Rev. Eddie K. Edwards, who taught me the importance of caring for widows – even before I became one.

Above all, we give thanks to God, our Father, our Maker and our Husband. (Isaiah 54:5).

"Religion that God our Father accepts as pure and faultless is this: to look after orphans and widows in their distress and to keep oneself from being polluted by the world." JAMES 1:27

TABLE OF CONTENTS

"God's Grace Bubble"

As I write this, I am approaching the fourth anniversary of my dear husband's transition to his heavenly home on July 25, 2004. His soul is resting in peace. And so is mine. It's all because of God's Grace Bubble. I won't say that this transition has been easy for me but, because of God's Grace Bubble, more things are going right than going wrong.

Every morning when I arise I say, "Lord, order my steps in your word today." And He does. Let me give you a few examples that I hope will help you understand the Grace Bubble.

Prior to my husband's departure, we had plans to move to Texas and had a lot of Texas clothing: hats, boots, jeans, etc. Well, after Rev. passed, it was hard for me to wear any of this clothing. However, one day not long after his departure, I prepared to dress. Very clearly, I heard the Lord say, "Put on your Texas garb." So I did, and left home headed for the post office.

Upon arriving at the post office and opening the box, there was only one little envelope inside. Had there been more mail, it could have easily been lost inside one of the papers. Then, again, it couldn't have been lost because it was a very special card. This is how it read: "Sorry, cowgirl, you lost your cowboy." My knees nearly buckled! Here I stood dressed in my western clothing and reading this sympathy note from someone I didn't know! I was determined to find out who this person was.

Immediately, I went back home and called Information to see if I could get a phone number for my sympathizer. Fortunately, the spelling of the name was unusual and I got the number and called. The lady on the other end told me how we had met. It was at a ladies' convention in Nashville, Tennessee, the year before. In a small group of ladies, I mentioned that my husband and I were going to move to Texas and be a cowboy and a cowgirl. When she heard that my husband had passed, she remembered our conversation. She had my business card and dropped her God-inspired card in the mail. That made my day. Just to know how God was watching over me and knew just what I needed is more than I can express.

Lord, how great Thou art! He had me dress for the occasion, and then He sent words of comfort to me through someone I didn't even know. This is just one example of God's Grace Bubble. Let me give you another one.

God often speaks to me in the shower. This is a place where He rains His shower of love down on me in the beginning of my day, following the reading of His word and prayer. Well, one morning He spoke to me and said: "Mary, because you have given so many people a new start in life, (that was the name of my family life ministry before I retired) I'm going to give you a new start in life."

Later that same day I opened up one of the sympathy cards that were steadily coming to my home. The one I want to tell you about had a cross on the outside and the words, "God Bless You" on the front. When I opened up the card, the words inside said, "Happy Birthday." The handwritten words on the bottom said, "We're praying for you." This couple probably grabbed the card hastily and thought it was a sympathy card. But I know differently. God had them send that card to confirm that He was going to give me a new start in life. Isn't that what a birthday is?

Not only did God put me in a Grace Bubble, He also gave me a new ministry for widows: www.widowswithwisdom.org. I've found that it takes a widow to know a widow. This isn't a ministry anyone would necessarily want. And it's not a club a woman would want to join unless there was a need. But I have learned to turn my grief into gratitude. And my sorrow has turned into joy because I have been given the opportunity to bring comfort to others such as myself who must learn how to live alone without our spouses.

Widow or not, God has a Grace Bubble for you also. His grace is sufficient for whatever you may be going through.

Caught Up In Him,

Minister Mary Darlene Edwards

INTRODUCTION

My name is Minister Mary Edwards. I am the Founder and President of Widows With Wisdom. It is my pleasure to share with you the information contained in this book. Join me as we transition from widowhood to womanhood – together. It takes a widow to know a widow.

When you think of the word "Widow," what comes to your mind? Many people, including some widows themselves, think of the words: lonely, pitiful, poor, dependent, a loser. Well, I'm here to tell you that not one of these adjectives describes me. In fact, I'm just the opposite. I guess it started when I was just a young girl…

When I was barely in my teens, I lost my virginity and became pregnant at the same time. It was said by society that I would be "just another negative welfare statistic." I recall thinking even then, "No. I'm better than that." Because of this positive attitude, I can say today that I've never been on welfare. I graduated with honors at the age of 16, with a three-year-old son. At the age of 18, I married for the first time. It was a difficult marriage that ended in divorce after 20years. As you can see, I don't give up easily.

I've received awards from the governmental offices of the City of Detroit, State of Michigan, County of Wayne, and even the President of The United States of America for my community achievements. The Women's Informal Network gave one of my most recent honors to me. They consider me to be "One of the Most Influential African-American Women in Metropolitan Detroit."

In 2004, after nearly 21 years of marriage to a wonderful man of God, Rev. Eddie K. Edwards, I became a widow. At the time of this teaching, I've been a widow for four years. This was my second 20-year marriage. In essence, except for four months of my life, I've never lived alone. Simply put, when I became a widow, I had to learn how to take care of myself quickly. And I did.

My motto is: "Learn. Do. Teach." So, here goes!

HOW WE GOT STARTED

The Bible tells us that, if we are watchful and prayerful, nothing comes upon us unawares. I know this from personal experience.

In January 2004, before I became a widow, I began to meet some very interesting widows. They were older women with great wisdom. One of them was Mother Melissa Davis, aka Mother Ruth. Mother Ruth was 93 years old at the time we met. I met Mother Ruth in a nail salon where she had a standing, that's right, standing appointment for every two weeks to get her fingers and toes groomed. Mother and I hit it off right away. I told her, "Mother when I grow up I want to be just like you." From that day to this, she calls me "Baby Ruth." Mother Ruth travels a great deal. Much of her travel is because she is sent for by large churches that want her to minister to them. Mother Ruth has outlived two husbands. The last time she got married she was 77 years old.

The second widow I met was Mother Ennis Byrdsong. Mother Byrdsong, age 85, has a perfect size 10 figure. She also has a personal fitness trainer and attends the fitness center at least twice a week. Mother Byrdsong is a nutrition specialist and takes absolutely no prescription medicines. She has written two books: her autobiography and a wonderful book on nutrition. Mother Byrdsong has a beau. He's 90 years old and she says he has perfect vision. "Doesn't even need reading glasses," so she says.

The third widow I met was Mother Ruthie Tate. Mother Tate came to me because she wanted to write a book. She was 79 at the time. Her birthday was coming up and she wanted to release her book by her 80th birthday, which she did. The title of her book is "God Made Morning Just For Me." She had her book signing at her 80th birthday party.

Needless to say, I found these widows to be intriguing. I was learning so much from them. So much so that in February 2004 I came home one day from visiting one of them and said to my husband, "Somebody needs to start a ministry and name it Widows With Wisdom." My husband and I laughed when he said, "Well, it won't be you. You're not a widow." It was a shock to all of us when one month later he was diagnosed with fourth stage cancer.

That was in March. In July he left for his heavenly home. And look at me now. You can be a wife in the morning and a widow in the afternoon.

As I said in the beginning, God prepares us for the future. If we are tuned into His voice, nothing will surprise us.

In August, one month after Rev. Edwards' departure, I had a support group meeting in my living room with about 15 widows present. It was easy to see that we needed a bigger place. Thus, we started meeting in the backroom of a local restaurant. In a short time, we outgrew that space as well. We now meet at the McDonnell Community Center at 24400 Civic Center Drive, Southfield, Michigan. Since our inception, we have embraced widows throughout Michigan, as well as Las Vegas, California, Louisiana, Ohio, New Mexico, Oklahoma, Louisiana, South and North Carolina, Alaska, Africa and Canada.

GIVE YOURSELF PERMISSION TO MOURN

A wife in the morning and a widow in the afternoon...

That's how fast my life changed. And it can happen to anyone. In fact, it has happened to 13 million widows in the United States alone. What do you do? Who do you turn to for the answers you need?

I had to learn quickly. My husband, Rev. Eddie K. Edwards, made his transition so fast that I wasn't prepared. However, I've learned a few things that might be helpful to you.

One of the first things you must do is:

GIVE YOURSELF PERMISSION TO MOURN.

It's okay to cry. In fact, I encourage you to do so. You will find that there is healing in tears. Regrettably, I didn't allow myself to cry. One month following my husband's death, I started a new ministry called Widows With Wisdom.

The reason I didn't allow myself to cry is because I was afraid that if I started I wouldn't be able to stop. In fact, I had cried so many tears during his illness I suspected that they had dried up. So, instead of spending a lot of time grieving, I busied myself reaching out to other widows.

Helping others is good. However, postponing a confrontation with your feelings by filling each day with frantic activity will only delay the grief process. Friends, the grief will remain until you deal with it.

Don't let anyone tell you how long you should grieve. It's different for everyone. But, if you don't seem to be handling it well, I encourage you to seek professional help. You may even want to join my support group. **www.widowswithwisdom.org**

BE AWARE OF A RANGE OF EMOTIONS

Losing a loved one – whether through unexpected or anticipated circumstances – is always traumatic. This is especially true with the death of a spouse. It is one of life's most profound losses. The transition from wife to widow to womanhood can be a very real, painful, personal, and sometimes overwhelming experience. The trauma of trying to adjust to this new identify, while being besieged with a multitude of urgent questions and decisions can be extremely difficult.

I've already spoken about the importance of giving yourself permission to mourn. Now let me give you another tip for today.

BE AWARE THAT YOU MAY EXPERIENCE A RANGE OF EMOTIONS

SHOCK...

NUMBNESS...

ANGER...

PAIN...

FEAR...

LONELINESS...

These may overlap each other. Grief does not proceed in an orderly fashion. One of the myths about mourning is that it has an ending point, that if you just wait long enough, it suddenly stops hurting. It doesn't. It requires work more than time, bereavement takes effort to heal. Mourning is a natural and personal process that's different for everyone. It cannot be rushed and it cannot happen without your participation. You must be willing to move on.

TIP: Take a 10-30 minute walk every day and while you walk. **<u>SMILE!</u>** It is the ultimate anti-depressant.

SEVEN STAGES OF GRIEF

It is widely accepted that there are seven distinct stages in the grieving process.

The seven stages of grief are:

- Shock or Disbelief
- Denial
- Bargaining
- Guilt
- Anger
- Depression
- Acceptance and Hope

Most people will see some if not all of the seven stages of grief in themselves as they grieve.

The first stage is obvious and I think we all see this in the first breaking of the news of a death or loss. We quite naturally are shocked and find the gravity of the situation difficult to take in.

Denial is the next stage of the grieving process and sometimes this stage will last only a moment and with others it may last for quite some time.

Each of the seven stages of grief will take different lengths of time to work through from person to person. Sometimes the first three stages may only last a moment and with others they could last for some considerable time.

Bargaining, although it may seem like a strange stage, is something that a lot of us do and has its roots in "what could I do to reverse the loss", "take me instead", this is quite natural and is an observed stage of grieving.

Guilt comes in and is very close to bargaining. One tends to blame themselves in an effort to reconcile the loss.

When anger occurs in the grieving process we know that the person is starting to come out of it. All of the stages up to this one have been very inward responses whereas anger is more of an outreach.

Depression is not so much a stage, it can come and go throughout the whole grieving process but when the anger stage is passed depression will also become less and less.

Finally acceptance and hope will return and marks the seventh stage of grief. At this point we understand that life will never be the same but we see hope and meaning in the future.

These seven stages of grief should not be taken as a hard and fast rule but more as an index of the stages of the grieving process.

The main point is that we can see our grief as a very natural process that we will work through from the initial shock to the eventual hope.

TIP: TAKE IT ONE DAY AT A TIME.

He Lives in My Arms

I thought Rev. Dr. Robert L. Redmond and I would grow old together. Instead, at the young age of 49, he died in my arms. My life, as I knew it, would never be the same. I was a happily married woman in the morning and a bereaved widow in the afternoon. On October 9, 2003, my widowhood journey began. My life was turned upside down and inside out.

Pastor Robert Redmond and I had grown up on the same street as teenage sweethearts, gotten married, and ministered side-by-side in the pastorate for 14 years. At the time of his departure, we had been married for 28 years. Before we had ministered to many. Now it was my time to be ministered to. The teacher needed to be taught, but who was equipped to handle the assignment? I didn't have that "superwoman," type-E (everything to everybody) will to continue on in the ministry. I wanted to pass the mantle on to the next person and become a support to them. My plan was to go home, turn out the lights, draw the blinds, and not interact with anybody or anything. Instead, I had to grieve in the public eye, even though I wanted time alone to mourn the memory of my dear departed husband. However, God had something else in mind.

In 2004, I received an invitation to come to a monthly Widows With Wisdom support group meeting, which convened at the home of Minister Mary Edwards. To my surprise, I learned that our husbands had common vision. Thus, Minister Edwards and I quickly began a beautiful relationship. I am impressed with this awesome woman of God whom I have seen up close and personal. Even though she had lost her husband, as I had, to this day I have never seen her burdened down with grief. Minister Mary's name is famed all across the country, yet she remains humble and focused on ministering to hurting widows and other women. She has served as an excellent role model and I wanted to become a part of her vision to help encourage other widows who face the same day-to-day challenges of having to live alone. My friend has taught me how to embrace life by extending a helping hand to a hurting heart. The compassion she has shown motivates me to want to give back to others who are making their transition from wife to widow.

Recently, Minister Mary asked me to speak at one of our widow's meetings. The theme was, "What is that in your hands?" With that thought in mind, I prayed and asked God to help me not only talk to the widows but also to do something my dear husband always encouraged us to do. I can hear him now saying, "Walk and Talk." In other words, put love in action.

I have always loved to sew. That's one of the gifts God has put in my hands. Fabric and a sewing machine.

Now, I'm able to make prayer shawls for the widows and others. Now, I'm able to spend time interceding for them in prayer.

As I drape my own shawl around my shoulders, it's as if the loving arms of God and my dear husband are embracing me. And, when my tears begin to fall upon my prayer shawl, I lift them up to heaven. The scriptures tell me they are placed in a vial as a sweet smelling fragrance to the Lord – not one of them is lost.

Perhaps one day I'll get married again. In the meantime, I will drape my prayer shawl around my shoulders and pray for widows who must learn to live without their spouses. But, spiritually speaking, we are not alone. Our Bible tells us that our Maker is our husband (Isa. 54:5). God is still alive.

And so is Robert L. Redmond's legacy, as I embrace his vision that he left with me.

Dr. Angela Redmond

Detroit, Michigan

FINANCIAL PROCESS

As a newly widowed person, there may be urgent financial and legal decisions you must make following the death of your spouse. Here you are trying to deal with your grief and the last thing you want to deal with is money matters. But money does matter, now and for your future. So try to do the best you can.

Know the stages of the financial process after the death of a spouse:

FIRST: you plan the funeral and consider immediate financial needs.

NEXT: After the funeral, you must gather financial documents and get benefits.

THEN: comes the stage to rebuild your financial life.

When it comes to finances, postpone any decisions that can be put off until you feel better emotionally. Don't make any major decisions for the first 90 days to six months after the funeral. Give yourself time. Many companies will grant you grace to get your paperwork in order.

Remember, everything has changed. Have a few trusted, knowledgeable people around you. There are many people who want to give you good advice but it may not fit your particular circumstances.

I've been blessed to have a team of advisors such as my pastor, attorney, accountant and prayer partners.

TIP: Sit in silence for at least 10 minutes each day. Let your mind and body rest.

FORGIVENESS

Today's message is not just for widows, but for anyone who finds themselves struggling with unforgiveness.

The night before my terminally ill husband went into the hospital, I got down before him on my knees, "Please forgive me for anything I've done to offend you," I asked him. A tear formed in my eye as I thought about the disagreements and little conflicts. Every argument, every time I felt slighted about some little thing or other, it all seemed so unimportant at that time. My husband forgave me.

The next day he went into the hospital. The doctors took one look at him and called Hospice Care the next day. Things were moving so fast.

The following night I was led by the Lord to spend the night alone with my husband. I sat up most of the night professing my love and appreciation to him for the things he had done for me, as well as for others. I also forgave him for the things he should have done but didn't do. Much of the night was spent in prayer, reading the scriptures to him. Although he was only half-conscious, I felt that he knew I was there.

Two years before his illness my husband had given me an alabaster box filled with the most beautiful fragrant oils. On the Sunday of his passing, I took the oils out of the alabaster box and anointed his feet with the oils. It was 11:00 a.m. At 6:25 p.m. on that day, he was escorted into his heavenly home.

God had me in a "grace bubble." And there was no unfinished business between my dear husband, Rev. Eddie K. Edwards and myself.

TIP: Forgive today. Tomorrow may be too late.

My Turn

I've been married, separated, divorced, remarried, and widowed. My second husband passed away April 19, 1988 and, at that time, I had two adolescent children. I promised them that now that they had lost their father, they did not have to worry about losing me. I promised them that I would not even date until they were "grown and gone." I told them that they were the center of my life and I would give them the best that I had – myself.

Time went by. The children all graduated from high school and went to college. I retired in 2005 from the Social Security Administration Department of the United States Government. Although I dated, not one of the fine gentlemen interested me enough to consider marriage. A lot of people were concerned that I had no serious male interest. Some even told me that my "dream man" wasn't real and that my standards were too high. Perhaps they were. But I knew what I wanted:

1. *He must respect women, not just the one he is with.*

2. *He must respect himself and have a strong self-image.*

3. Be self-confident, easy to talk to, honest, and gentle.
4. Have a good sense of humor and a lot of integrity.
5. Love to listen.

Even my children kept asking me why I didn't like anyone, or why I was running off the men who liked me. None of them understood. I had gotten to the point of enjoying being alone and I didn't mind waiting.

However, waiting came to an end in January 2005 when I met Mr. DuBois Ross, a Tuskegee Airman. We met at a church in Detroit where I was serving as a volunteer speaker for a Healthy Living Project for my former employer, Social Security Administration. Mr. Ross helped me carry in my display. From the very beginning, I knew he was quite a gentleman. That has proven to be true.

We went inside the church together. I enjoyed talking to him, as well as listening to him. I started thinking: "This man is too good to be true." But it was somewhat disturbing to me when he said that he graduated from Hampton University in 1941. I wasn't even born in 1941! So then I decided that he must have been a child prodigy and graduated from college at 15. He didn't appear to be that much older than I. I could work with that.

A word of advice to widows and other women: I don't think women should look for men. I think women should get lost in their own lives and be found by the man. I think it is more important to be the right person rather than to find the right person. So I would advise women to get lost in becoming a better person so they can then be found.

Well, because I waited, God helped my dream man find me. My relationship with him has blossomed from the day we met to this day. And, as the saying goes, "Age is just a number." DuBois and I have had numerous loving and exciting days, as we grow older – together.

Ernestine P. Stewart

Southfield, Michigan

TAME OUR FEARS

My thoughts now are the need to:
TAME OUR FEARS

If you are living alone, there are several simple and inexpensive things you can do to maintain a feeling of security.

- Give a spare house or apartment key to a trusted family member or friend;
  OR:
- Conceal a spare key outside your home and tell a friend or family member where the key is located. Use your ingenuity but don't be too cleaver, A key that you, your family or trusted friend, can't find defeats the purpose. Don't draw attention to yourself as you conceal the key.

  Personal story: *I hid an extra key in my backyard. I'll never forget the day I had to use it. I forgot the exact area where the key was hidden and dug up a large portion of my backyard trying to find it. I never did.*

- Install timers on a TV or radio and on several conspicuous lights throughout your home. Set the timers for when you will be away from home and when you expect to come into an empty house after dark. Timers cost less than $20 and can be purchased at a hardware store or home improvement center. They are easy to install and set.

- Place a spare car key in a magnetic key box and attach the box to a concealed but accessible spot on the outside of your car. Again, don't attract attention to yourself as you conceal the key box. Magnetic key boxes cost less than $2.00 and can be purchased at a car wash.
- Consider a pet, not just for security but for companionship as well.

REMEMBER: Life isn't fair, but it is still good.

ANGER

Recently a widow was released from prison after spending 2½ years behind bars for something she didn't do. She had been given a life sentence for poisoning her husband. It was reported that her conviction was based primarily on her bizarre behavior following the death of her husband. A DNA examination proved that she was innocent. Thank God for DNA!

Indeed, the lost of a spouse is one of the most devastating experiences a husband or wife will have during their lifetime. All of us are capable of acting "abnormal." At times like these, the fine line between sanity and insanity can be very, very fine – almost non-existent. Some of our behavior may even be defined as "crazy."

During the early stages of my own widowhood, I did something that was misunderstood. There was some open criticism from those close to me. Quite frankly, their attitudes made me angry. Anger is a common emotion following the loss of a loved one.

When I was confronted with a false accusation, I really wanted to lash out at the person. But then I remembered something a wise woman once said to me. *"Honey, when someone pushes you down in the mud, don't try to wipe it off while it is wet. That will only make matters worse. It will smear. Wait until it dries and it will fall off by itself.*" Those words have been one of my most cherished lessons. Let it be yours as well.

TIP: DNA can prove a person's guilt or innocence. Wait it out. DNA can also be a reminder that we DON'T NEED ANGER.

Widows
With Wisdom
"A Holy Hookup"

As soon as I received it, I listened to the entire CD, "Transition: From Widowhood to Womanhood," in my car. It was very good. I especially like the topics on finances, children, and dating. It was quite a challenge for me to begin going out to functions by myself when I became a widow. The Holy Spirit has been my comforter and teacher in that area. Now, I travel and simply enjoy life.

I was also very apprehensive about dating, but God brought a special young man into my life and I learned so much about relationships. It was quite difficult, however, when the relationship ended. But, once again, I learned a lot about myself, and it was another opportunity for me to grow and to be able to minister to others in an area I was very unfamiliar with.

After my husband died, I also made some very unwise choices in the area of finances. And eight years later, I'm in the process of rebuilding.

Also, my sons were ages 13 and 15 at the time of their father's death, and I remember crying out to God about them not having a father. God promised to be their father, but I had to let go. My grip on them was so tight and I was in God's way. Since the day that I obeyed and let my sons go, I've watched them grow into magnificent towers of strength and faith. They are now 20 and 22 years old, and I'm blessed beyond measure. I look forward to becoming a part of Widows With Wisdom. I agree that this is a "Holy Hookup."

LuWanna Pruitt
Saginaw, Michigan

SHOULD I MOVE

Before my husband became ill and passed, we had plans to sell our home and move out of state. His passing put an entirely different perspective on things. Moving to another state without him wouldn't be the same. I prayed carefully about this matter and consulted with family and friends. God made it clear to me that moving out of state wasn't part of His plan for me. Take time before making such a drastic move. Too much change too soon isn't good.

However, you may want to downsize. If so, don't move too fast

Even under normal circumstances, moving can be very stressful. Visit some of your single and/or widowed friends. Ask them questions about where they are living. But keep in mind that what may be right for them won't necessarily be right for you. Each individual is different and has different needs. You may want to stay where you are and bring in a family member or boarder to share your home with you.

Whether or not you move, remember no matter how you feel, get up, dress up, and show up.

WHAT DO I DO WITH HIS CLOTHING?

This was a real problem for me because my husband was big in spirit but small in statue. Plus, he was the GQ Mayor. In other words, he had three closets of clothing, hats, shoes, boots, etc.

Many people were interested in purchasing his clothes but they weren't the right size. Thus, they laid in our bedroom across our bed for several months, while I slept in the guest room. Finally, I just had my church come and take them away. This was very painful for me. While I did keep a few sentimental items, I encourage you to get rid of things that you can't personally use.

Don't let your home become a shrine in your husband's memory. He's gone, but you are still here and you must get on with your life. Memories are very important, but they cannot be used as a shield against the present. At some point in your grieving, you will be ready to try to say goodbye.

Finally, ladies, love and listen to your children, but don't let them run your life. They have good intentions and motives, but don't stop your life to please their whims.

TIP: It is very important that you have a reason to get up in the morning.

So, I encourage you to wake up in the morning and complete the following statement, **"My purpose today is to_____** *(fill in the blank.)*

"WHERE'S DAD?"

Over one million children lose one or both of their parents to death by the age of 15. Fortunately, when my spouse passed, our children were all adults and on their own. However, we did have grieving grandchildren. Let me encourage you not to get so caught up in your own grief that you forget the needs of the little ones who have lost their beloved father or grandfather.

Don't wait for questions from the child. As soon as death seems imminent, or as soon as possible after a sudden death, approach the subject. Do it yourself if you are the parent, grandparent or guardian.

Think about what you want to say ahead of time. It's okay to cry but keep in mind that your child is not your confidant. Don't burden the child. Keep in mind that they more than likely will go through the same stages of grief that you go through. You and the child or children may need grief counseling during this crisis. Even if you don't have insurance to cover the expense, check with your medical doctor, local church, or even the school to find counseling.

Here are some guidelines for supporting your children or grandchildren during this crisis.

Have the children:

- Draw a picture of the way they are feeling today.
- Draw a picture depicting a favorite activity the children shared with the family member who dies.
- Create a collage with photos and other objects that remind them of their favorite times with the family member who dies.

Older children and adolescents can express their grief not only through art projects such as these but also through writing about their feelings and experiences. You can suggest any one of the following writing activities to your children.

Have them:

- Write a letter in which he expresses how much he misses the family member who died or says farewell to this person if he wasn't able to do so before death.
- Write a story in which he relates a favorite memory to the family member who died his changing feelings and thoughts.

For more ways to help grieving children, I recommend you get a copy of the book, <u>Grieving for Dummies</u>, by Greg Harvey, PhD. Don't let this title offend you. It's an excellent, practical guide for coping with the loss of a love one.

Keep your eyes and ears open to be sure the children are experiencing normal grieving behavior and aren't falling into acting out and depression.

If you see evidence of this, be sure to get professional counseling.

TIP: Your children are worth close supervision!

Changing Lanes

What is this you say about "Changing Lanes?" Well, life throws so many curves at us that it is nearly impossible to keep up with them. You look around, and things seem normal; but once you take your focus off the clear vision in front of you, you may wind up in a 360-degree turn. I am explaining to you the scenario of my life. I have encountered life, death, hope and peace in the midst of what is going on around me. I have to begin by taking you on a journey that will trigger some emotions in you that you may have not connected with in quite a while.

In the fall of 2003, I was a wife and a nursing mom of a one-year old daughter. Lo and behold, at that time, I was experiencing migraine headaches for about two and a half months that would not go away. On September 7th, I had a ruptured aneurysm. I was in a coma and the physicians expressed to my family that I would not survive. The doctors gave no hope in the situation. The physicians mentioned that if I did make it, I would be a "vegetable" at most. I was able to overcome the statistical diagnosis that was thrown at me. I managed to successfully complete occupational, physical and speech therapies consecutively. Due to a few seizures after surgery and treatment, I had another aneurysm detected at the end of October 2003. I was scheduled for another surgery on November 9th to remove it. After my husband's persistence, prodding and searching, he was able to get me to the "top surgeon" of Neurology at The Johns Hopkins Hospital located in Baltimore, Maryland. The surgery was very successful. After a repeated round of occupational, physical and speech therapies, I was finally through with this nightmare on December 10th, 2003.

Now in 2004, during my recovery, my husband Reggie did a lot of walking to relieve stress from being my sole caregiver, and from also being a stay-at-home father. All of a sudden Reggie developed a small lump in his left thigh. There was nothing to worry about at that particular time because there was no pain being caused by this lump. It was not until May 2005, that Reggie began to develop sharp pains in his left leg. His primary physician at the time referred him to a surgeon to have the lump removed. The surgeon told me at the end of the surgery that the lump was malignant. The cancer is a very rare type called Lipo-Sarcoma (soft tissue cancer). This was our second turn of events, which took Reggie from being my caregiver to my becoming his sole caregiver. We were now entering what was to become the wildest ride of our lives. We dealt with radiation treatment for the last six months of 2005. The physician handling Reggie's case for this treatment felt he was doing fine at the end of November. Reggie was discharged because there were no outward symptoms to tell us otherwise. He felt great, and his energy was returning. We were looking forward to bigger and better things in life.

I was on a roll come the summer of 2006. I directed a summer youth camp and I was moving forward, but… the CANCER came back!! Reggie's health began to whirlwind again out of control. This time the cancer had metastasized to his back and right rib area. Reggie was in so much pain at this point that he could not lie down or stand up. Oh, what turmoil! I became a caregiver for a second time after about 18 months. Yes, my life had to make some major adjustments, because Reggie could not get around much by himself, and our daughter who was now four years old, started helping me out as much as she possibly could. Reggie went through radiation and chemotherapy treatments to help relieve the pain and to shrink the tumors. I think that we all were burnt out from getting up early in the mornings, traveling to the hospital and then ending our days just tired from "sickness."

In October 2007, when Reggie learned that the cancer had metastasized even more to his liver and right lung, he said, "enough is enough already!!" He refused to have any more radiation or chemotherapy treatments. He was very tired of the routine. Who could blame him? There was absolutely nothing I could do but be a supportive wife and caregiver. When the late spring of 2008 rolled around, (the beginning of June), Reggie could take the pain he was experiencing no longer. He agreed to one treatment of chemotherapy to shrink a tumor, which had metastasized to his abdomen. Reggie asked me how I felt about his decision to have the treatment. There was nothing I could say, because I was actually in shock. I told him that if he felt that the treatment would help I was all for it.

At this point, Reggie did not talk much about his body's changes or his aches and pains. My husband was a very strong individual. In fact, he prided himself on not allowing people to see or hear him complain about how much his body was hurting. On July 11, 2008, Reggie was admitted to hospice care, where he resided until his death three weeks later.

I now sit in a position where my life has taken yet another change. I am now a widow and a single parent. Within the past five years, my changing lanes have been critical, abrupt, and transforming. I have undertaken situations, which most people will never encounter in their lifetime. BUT THE GOOD NEWS IS: LIFE WILL GO ON, and I now have the courage, the determination, and the self will to continue moving forward wherever life's "lane changes" will take me next.

Angela Timpson
Dayton, Ohio

HOW TO HANDLE STRESS

We've been speaking about the need to give yourself permission to mourn, the range of emotions we experience, the various stages of the financial process after the death of a spouse, how to tame our fears, what to do with our late husband's clothing, whether or not we should move, and how to help our children with their grief.

Now I want to talk about:

HOW TO HANDLE STRESS

Have you been allowing someone to get on your LAST nerve? The one you were saving for yourself? If so, beware. Stress can wreak havoc on your health.

Guarding your health can be among the least of your concerns during your time of grief. But you must work toward maintaining your health as soon as you feel able. This means beginning some form of regular exercise, getting proper nutrition, and reporting physical complaints to your doctor.

Here are a few tips to help reduce stress. This can work for anyone.

PREPARE FOR BED

1. Start with a bubble bath and some candles and light music.
2. Tape your late night shows so you can get more sleep. I watched a lot of CNN during

my initial stages of widowhood. However, I found that I could sleep a lot better with the lights and sounds from the television turned off.

3. Instead of watching television all night, tune into some easy listening, soothing music. And/or read a good book. Perhaps even the Bible.

4. One of the worse things you can do is watch the 11:00 p.m. news before trying to go to sleep. I don't think I need to tell you why.

TIP: Pray and/or meditate on the goodness of God. Trust Him to lead the way and take care of you.

REDUCING STRESS

I'd like to share more on reducing stress. This is my top-ten checklist for reducing stress every day.

1. Pray. Go to bed on time. Get up on time so you can start the day unrushed.
2. Allow extra time to do things and to get to places.
3. Pace yourself. Spread out big changes and difficult projects over time. Don't lump the hard things all together.
4. Take one day at a time.
5. Do something for the child in you every day. For example, get a coloring book and color outside of the lines just for the fun of it. Go to the playground and swing or slide down the sliding board. *(Forget the monkey bars!)*
6. Carry a Bible or another good book with you to read between appointments or while waiting in line.
7. Listen to a tape while driving that can help improve your quality of life.
8. Write down thoughts and inspirations. Every day, find time to be alone.
9. Every night, before bed, think of one thing you're grateful for that you've never been grateful for before. Write it down.

10. Don't listen to the late night news. It can be depressing

TIP: Never borrow from the future. If you worry about what may happen tomorrow and it doesn't happen, you have worried in vain. Even if it does happen, you will have worried twice.

Taking Help

After the death of my husband Don, I was at a loss. He went so quickly.

It was tax time and I was fearful. He had done our tax filings for all of our 27 years of marriage. His death in January made tax time only a few months away. Every time the mail came, and a tax envelope arrived, I wondered, "Who will do this? I don't know how to file these papers." I felt panicky.

Don enjoyed doing the tax filings. He enjoyed telling our children what little refunds they would receive. I possessed none of his traits and talents. I prayed daily for help.

One day I received a telephone call from his brother Gene. "If there is anything I can do for you, just let me know."

Like all the other parting words, I felt these obligatory gestures were not really true, bona fide offers to be accepted. As a new widow, I felt helpless, alone, and vulnerable for the first time.

Swallowing my pride, I felt I really should consider taking Gene up on this offer because tax time was nearing. But first I'll try a CPA firm. I asked God for help. Failing to get a response from the CPA firm I called, I decided to take the risk and see if Gene was sincere.

Afraid I would burst into tears, I decided to email Gene and ask him if he really wanted to help. He responded quickly by email, stating he not only meant it, but he immediately called me on the telephone to make arrangements. He said he and his wife would come and spend a day with the children and me. He wanted me to locate all the papers in advance to expedite things.

My sweetheart, true to form, had shown me where to look for the tax papers, ("...just in case...nothing is going to happen, but if it does..." he assured me). There they were, all neatly filed away, and labeled from past years. Through my pain, I also had the sensibility to put all tax notices I had received in a single file.

I felt such relief to have all the papers Gene called for on the day he and his wife arrived. I was so proud that I had learned something from my darling husband--to be orderly when it came to important paperwork.

After exchanging pleasantries, Gene went busily to the task. He went 'on line' on our computer, and showed his nephew how to file electronically. My son didn't hesitate and wasn't fearful at all. He gladly dove right in and filed not only his but his sisters taxes, too. I was so thrilled to hear my son laugh, for it had been awhile since I heard that familiar sound. I was glad that he had a tutor in his uncle, who did things just like his dad.

That day God had not only made a way for me to have this dreaded task behind me, but He also gave my family a moment of love in time of need.

Task completed, they gathered their things. I choked back tears, as they drove away. Gene wouldn't take any money. He said, "No, this is what a brother does for his family, and my brother would have done it for me." I sighed with such relief. I was restored again to normalcy even if I was a new widow.

I was happy God had sent His servants to minister to me and mine. I am now looking forward to next year's tax season.

My advice to the widows: Don't be too prideful. Do take the hand when it is extended and seek out help. If you fear, ask God to guide you. He will do it. God will make a way and anoint the person for helping us in our time of need. That is what the church is supposed to do, take care of the widows and orphans. (James 1:27)

Marilyn Bread

Elgin, Oklahoma
A Widow and spouse of Jesus,
since January 1, 2008

In Loving Memory of
My Beloved Husband

Geoffrey John Bernardo

"Thank you, Mommy, you are my best friend," said my two plus-year-old daughter Phoebe, giving me a warm kiss when I was feeling so doggone tired cleaning up the house and looking after her for the whole day. I was stunned. I know she speaks a lot better now, better than the other kids at her age, but the idea to say such a thought convinced me that she is really from the heaven. Perhaps she understands. Perhaps she just imitates the cartoons she watches everyday, I don't know. But I have no doubt she is a person with a big heart.

She is a cutie; she is adorable; she is keeping me alive after her daddy, my beloved husband, passed away last year, 2005, just a week after her first birthday, which we planned to celebrate together with her Auntie, Grandma and Grandpa. His so-sudden-death made my world upside down. Our marriage was not even two years old yet. He is already gone. I couldn't stop crying but the Lord keeps every single tear I poured out. He cares.

More than one year now my husband gone. He constantly came to me into dreams, looked so real. If I could ask him to come back to the earth, probably he doesn't want to. He is so much happier now, living with the Lord. But The Lord doesn't forsake me.

I will not leave you as orphans; I will come to you. - John 14:18

Never will I leave you; never will I forsake you. - Hebrews 13:5

Even though I can't see the Lord physically, I could feel His presence even stronger now. I lost my earthly husband but I got a greater husband, a Heavenly Husband and Father.

Today I could laugh and enjoy my life again, but my grief will never be over. It's just getting better everyday because The Lord helps mend it. I even managed to write a book about my life with my husband. I want Phoebe to know her daddy better through this book once she grows older and understands more. I want it to be the best treasure Phoebe will have in her life.

Being a new young widow is not easy but I'm definitely not alone. Getting to know the other widows and their life stories would be great. We could support and strengthen each other. Prayers, encouragements, advices, testimonies, many more, could lift up our burdens.

I have been looking for some websites about young Christian widows. Nothing came up. So with my limited knowledge of website building, I have a call to create this simple website to give the place for young Christian widows to share, to laugh, to listen, to cheer-up, to give and seek advice and most of all is to keep praising the Lord in need and in want.

**"There is a time for everything,
and a season for every activity
under heaven..." - Ecclesiates 3:1.**

Yes, everything in this world happens at its own time, including when the Lord is going to call us home. It is my joy to know where my husband is now. I am crying because I am missing him so much but I am joyful and looking forward to the time when I will see him again in the BIGGEST reunion ever in the clouds when our Lord comes back for us.

Vita Bernardo

Oakville, Ontario, Canada

www.joyofchristianwidows.com

This is our Canadian widow's website. Take time to look at it and drop her a line. It is a beautiful site!

HANDLING CAR REPAIRS

"Oh, no! What's that noise I hear?"

Shortly after burying my husband, I had car trouble. Not only were my spirits low, but my finances were low and my knowledge of car repairs was next to nothing. There were some things I had to learn on my own.

As a point of reference, $82 billion a year is spent on car repairs. Much of that is spent by women and widows. So let me give you a few simple tips:

First of all, you want to get towing service ahead of time.

Be sure to read the Service Warranty Manual. It's probably in your glove compartment of the car.

Then decide whether you should go to the dealer or to an independent car repair shop. Go to the dealer, if the car is still under warranty, or if there is a recall on your automobile. Wherever you go, be specific when you describe your problem. What? When? Where? How did it happen?

Once you decide where to take the car, ask to see the worn parts to be sure they were replaced, if necessary. You are entitled to this. In fact, the new car dealer will give them to you without asking.

Get a second opinion.

Be sure to have a cell phone, especially if you drive on the highway.

Take a "powder puff car repair class." Sometimes you can find them at your community center or local community college.

Keep a battery charger in the car. That may be all you need.

Finally, be careful whom you ask for help.

Don't Be A Weeping Widow

Minister Mary Edwards has commented on the despair we often feel in dealing with widowhood. We have our good days and then we have "our moments," especially during the early stages when you just cry, cry, cry. Suddenly it came to me that GOD does not want us to be "weeping widows" like the weeping willow tree; with its leaves downcast, being tossed to and fro with the wind. We don't want to be seen always with our heads downcast, a sad countenance, and a "woe is me" spirit.

The Lord led me to Psalm 137, where the children of Israel were in captivity and they wept when they remembered Zion. We weep when we remember sometimes our lives when we were married. How we once had husbands who loved and took care of their families, fixed leaky faucets, and our cars. Yes, we remember. The children of Israel were so sad, they began to hang their harps in the willow trees and ask the question, "How shall we sing the Lord's song in a strange land?" Widowhood is a strange land that we have never traveled before. It is a place in our lives that is new and often bewildering. How can we have joy in the midst of sorrow?

The Lord never wants us to stop praising Him. The Bible says, "The joy of the Lord is your strength." So, praise is never out of season. Psalm 30:5 says, "Weeping may endure for a night, but joy cometh in the morning."

Now's the time to take those classes that we need to complete our degrees. Now's the time to expand our horizons, travel to new territories, and meet new people. Now's the time for us to be more like Anna the prophetess and widow who spent her time in the temple fasting and praying. She was so busy in the church that she was blessed to see the Messiah.

So, we must gird up our loins and move forward, as difficult as it may seem sometimes. In Hebrews 13:5 the Lord says, "I will never leave you nor forsake you." Therefore, regardless of how strange and foreboding the land of widowhood seems, the Lord will be with us. You never realize how much you need and depend upon the Lord until you become a widow, but GOD is always faithful. Widows, be encouraged to lift up those "hung down heads" and stay with the Lord. As Dottie Peoples says, "You Can Begin Again." And certainly you can with GOD as your eternal partner. May GOD bless you.

Mrs. Marva Dozier

River Rouge, Michigan
Widow of Norman Dozier
October 12, 1940 – October 22, 2001

Divine Connection

I am convinced that God allows us to meet people at a set time, a set place, and for a set plan in our lives, in order that we may accomplish the purpose that He has given us for His Kingdom.

There are various means by which we can meet people and the Internet or web is one that allows us to learn, communicate and bring people together - even thousands of miles away. Technology is changing and every generation has to keep up with it. Using this method has been a blessing in my life.

Speaking of my life, it has been a journey. I grew up as an only child. In July 1981, I lost my father and in January 2001, I lost my mother but God connected me with someone who was there for me like a mother and helped me through my grief.

In January 2003, my husband left home that morning for work and the next time I saw him was on a hospital table dead. He was only 52 years old and I immediately became a widow and a single parent.

Just when I was beginning to accept this reality, Hurricane Katrina came in and not only flooded my home and my parent's home, but destroyed all of our sentimental things.

The word "overwhelmed" became the simple answer to the #1 question- "How are you doing?" When I felt overwhelmed, I would go to the Word of God and pray and read Psalm 61:2.

" ... when my heart is overwhelmed: lead me to the rock that is higher than I."

Other words like faith, rest, favor, eagle, wisdom and widow became a part of my word study. I would ask many questions like: "Where is the church. I need help. Have they not read James 1:27, Deut. 24:17, Isa. 1:17, I Timothy 5: 3-8?" "God, do you see me?" "Why did you take my husband, who was a contractor, when you knew that a flood was coming?" Every time I get to the point where I feel I can't take anymore, God speaks to me through scripture, songs, and through other ministers.

I heard and played songs over and over like, "Encourage Yourself in the Lord," "Rest in Him," "He's Faithful," and so many more. My mirror was used often to help me speak faith confessions to myself. My praise and worship would get so awesome in the car while driving to work that many times I felt like pulling over and having a Holy Ghost party all by myself and the AWESOME 3.: Father, Son and Holy Ghost.

In 2007, I had this need to find my purpose in the midst of all this mess. My life and actions had to line up with what I was saying and what I said I believed. Kingdom living and life had to be first. I had to choose to be an eagle or a chicken in the midst of this storm. So I began to search the web about widows and widows' ministries. My life became my message because I began to meet so many ladies who were widows and even some that came into my life and were later widows. "God, what are you telling me?"

In my prayer time, I began to seek him more about my purpose. He brought back teachings that I heard years ago about being an "able body minister." Then I started receiving newsletters again from David Wilkerson, from Times Square Church in New York. He is a pastor that I have never met, but God has used his sermons since 1994 to feed me in some tough times in my life so that I could help someone else.

> **"Who comforteth us in all our tribulations,**
> **that we may be able to comfort them which**
> **are in any trouble, by the comfort wherewith**
> **we ourselves are comforted of God." (2**
> **Corinthians 1: 3-4)**

As I continued to seek the Kingdom of God and pray, He started showing and confirming to me my purpose: to minister to and empower the widow.

Of all the webs I looked at, and people I spoke with, it wasn't until May 8, 2008 that God spoke to my heart to reply on the web to "Widows with Wisdom," headed by Minister Mary Edwards in Detroit.

www.widowswithwisdom.org.

One confirmation was the title song - my song - on her page that immediately starts ministering to you - "Encourage Yourself in the Lord." That past week, I had been playing that song over and over. The next confirmation came when I learned from the website that she reads David Wilkerson's sermons also. And, after speaking to her, she expressed how she also enjoys his messages and how anointed they are. When I shared with Minister Edwards that I was going to start my widows' support group in my living room, she confirmed that's also how she started.

All of this started from a few words in response to a web page. The "connection" started right away and has moved to long, exciting conversations and prayers of agreement. She has encouraged me with her wisdom, vitality, her faith in God and her joyful attitude. I have been able to focus more on my purpose and less on my problems. Worry only worships the words of the enemy.

"But seek ye first the kingdom of God, and his righteousness; and all these things shall be added unto you..." (Matthew 6: 25-34)

I'm believing, expecting, trusting, depending and straining to see what the AWESOME 3 is going to do next. So I encourage you to Get Connected because HELP IS ON THE WAY.

Sherryl Williams
Gretna, Louisiana

SOULFUL LIVING

HE WAS YOUR SOULMATE...
YOU MET HIM
YOU DATED HIM
YOU FELL IN LOVE WITH HIM
YOU CARED FOR HIM
IN SICKNESS AND IN HEALTH
BUT...
HE MADE HIS TRANSITION
FROM THIS LIFE
AND
YOU ARE STILL HERE

NOW, IT'S YOUR TURN
IT'S YOUR TURN
FOR SOME SOULFUL LIVING
IT'S TIME TO
LOVE AND CARE FOR YOURSELF
IT'S TIME TO LAUGH
IT'S TIME TO DO SOME SOULFUL LIVING!
THERE'S NOTHING TO IT BUT TO DO IT
LOVE
LAUGH
LIVE

A LIVING LEGACY

"Sons are a heritage from the Lord. Children a reward from Him." (Psalm.127:3)

Because I know very little about my family history, heritage is extremely important to me. While some parents name their girls Tracey, Stacey, Lacey, and Nancy, if I had a girl today, I would name her "LEGACY."

Since my husband's departure, I have endeavored to keep his memory alive. By doing this, his family, friends and associates, as well as any new offspring that may come along, will know that he was a man who impacted his generation and was very special to us.

My husband started his ministry in 1976 delivering food baskets to widows. Caring for widows and orphans has always been very important to us. That's one of the reasons I've crafted this and other resource materials.

He also loved to decorate the Christmas tree all by himself. Visitors would come during the holiday season "just to see Eddie's tree." He was so proud of that tree. Every year he trimmed it in a different color. This year I plan to make a picture Christmas card of him with HIS tree!

With this thought in mind, you may want to keep your husband's memory alive in a special way. If so, here's a short list of remembrances you can create to help you recollect and celebrate your loved one's life.

Create a picture album or book that chronicles the milestones in your loved one's life, including major accomplishments and relationships.

Create a collage or montage that uses images, tokens, keepsakes, and mementos that represent your loved one's best qualities and highest interests.

Establish a living memorial. The most popular form of living memorials is the living tree memorial. For this kind of memorial, you arrange to have a tree planted in honor of your loved one in a nature preserve or on some public land. Our ministry has a summer camp. I plan to have a tree planted on that land.

There are so many other suggestions you can refer to. Please pick up a copy of the book I spoke of earlier, <u>Grieving for Dummies</u>, by Greg Harvey, PhD.

A NEW YOU

When you come out of widowhood and move back into womanhood varies from woman to woman. Many of you have spent a portion of your lives caring for your late spouses. In the process, you have neglected your own well-being. However, at the end of the day, whenever that day may be, I want you to consider a "New Start in Life." In other words, do something good for yourselves.

How about some quick beauty and fashion tips to help you feel great fast.

1. Brighten up your room with fresh flowers, which you can get inexpensively at a wholesaler or at your grocery store. Treat yourself to a bouquet and place them in the room where you spend the most time. Your mood will brighten every single time you walk into that room!

2. The same goes for candles. What's your most favorite scent – chances are that there's a candle to go with it. Just like flowers, candles don't have to be expensive; there are wonderful scents available at your local grocery store or discount retailer.

3. Treat YOU! Not too many of us can afford an entire new wardrobe – but what about a blouse, a pair of jeans, or a cute new

handbag or a fabulous new pair of shoes (all of which can be gotten inexpensively). This season, COLOR is everywhere – hot blues, vibrant greens, lemon yellow...all are great mood-lifters AND look great on every skin tone. We're still seeing a lot of oversize handbags, but clutches are also HUGE. My passion is SHOES! No matter your taste, there's a shoe for you. From sky-high stilettos to ballerina flats; from wedges to gladiator-style sandals, there truly is "something for everyone"!

4. And while you're paying attention to you, how about "switching up" your look a little bit? When was the last time that you had a professional manicure or pedicure? Choose a wonderful color; perhaps one that you've never tried before (note: red, pink, hot orange or the "French, which is so popular.) Show off wonderful YOU! When was the last time you did something different to or with your hair? No, don't go cutting it all off or going platinum if you're dark brown...but how about some highlights – or perhaps a headband; another hot accessory. The ponytail also continues to be very popular for both day and evening. Just a little tiny change goes such a long way to refresh and renew.

5. Want to lose five pounds fast? Cut out some of the carbs, sweets! And late night snacks.

<u>Remember</u> – when you take the time to pay just a little bit of attention to you and to your environment, your spirit and your mood are going to naturally lift – go ahead and give it a try!

DATING

At some point on your widowhood journey, you may want to start dating. In case this feels strange to you, let me give you a few tips. I don't want you to be as naïve as one of my widow friends. She was invited to go out to dinner by a fine gentleman. Instead of saying "yea" or "nay," she said, "I'm not hungry." She didn't realize he was asking for a date. Fortunately, he asked her again and she said "yes." Now they are a twosome.

So, let's get to some rules:

RULE #1 – LISTEN TO YOUR GUT

It's important to pay attention and listen to your gut. If a potential date's actions or words set off an internal alarm system, you owe it to yourself to pay attention and act accordingly. These alarms can be both good and bad. For example, if you met someone online and they seem interesting, then you talk to them on the phone and they sound completely different (in a negative way), you may decide not to meet them in person. A positive example would be if you were on a date with someone and they seemed nervous but well intentioned, your gut might tell you to give them a second chance. By going on a second date, you'll gain a better understanding of who they really are and if you'd like to see them again.

RULE #2 – PAY ATTENTIN TO RED FLAGS

Oftentimes this alarm system is turned way down. As a result, we often ignore red flags and find ourselves getting involved with inappropriate partners because we're not paying attention. To become a truly successful single in the new millennium, you owe it to yourself to become a red flag specialist. That means paying attention to red flags as they are presented to you on dates. For example, I'm not a smoker and I don't like to be around smokers. If I went out on a date and the guy lit up a cigarette after dinner, that would be the end of the relationship before it got started! Another example of a red flag would be if you found yourself on a date with someone who could not stop talking about his former or deceased wife. He may be a fantastic person, and eventually make a great partner, but right now he's not ready. Your job is to pay attention to that red flag and not pursue them.

I want to spend more time here because I've seen some horrible things happen to widows because they were misled or lonely.

BEWARE OF SCAMS
A SLICK AND A PROMISE

Much of my time is spent counseling women and widows. Earlier this week, I received a telephone call from a widow out of state. She was deeply depressed. Her husband had passed just a couple of years ago. He left her a large inheritance and, in a short time, she had been robbed of all of her money - not with a gun, but by what I call "A Slick and a Promise."

My friend had been married for a long time. He was her childhood sweetheart. When her husband passed, she was lonely and afraid. She didn't know how to date. So, when she was asked out, she accepted. Before she knew it, he had romanced her right out of her money.

Devastated from this scam, she had a nervous breakdown, a heart attack, and eventually she attempted suicide. Thank God she didn't succeed!

Without going into further detail, let this serve as a warning to you or someone you know. We are living in a world gone mad. There are wolves out there in the highways and the byways dressed in sheep clothing. They are just waiting for naive women (and men) to take advantage of. In the process of one of these "slicks with a promise" getting over, some unsuspecting victim gets betrayed and crushed. Not only is this widow grieving the loss of her life partner, but also her inheritance. It's going to take her a long, long time to pick up the pieces of her life and put them back together again.

Beloved, get a good, honorable financial advisor.

BOOK and RESOURCE LIST

These are suggestions only. We have not read them all... many have been recommended to us.

- <u>A Journey of Hope</u>, by Grace Wulff
- <u>Living through the Loss of Someone You Love</u>, by Sandra Aldrich
- <u>From One Single Mother to Another</u>, by Sandra Aldrich
- <u>Beginnings – A Book for Widows</u>, by Betty Jane Wylie
- <u>To Live Again</u> by Catherine Marshall
- <u>Meeting God at Every Turn</u>, by Catherine Marshall
- <u>Through the Wilderness of Loneliness</u>, by Tim Hansel
- <u>God In the Dark</u>, by Lucy Shaw
- <u>Let Me Grieve But Not Forever</u>, by Verdell Davis
- <u>A Grief Observed</u>, by C.S. Lewis (one of the best, a classic on grief)
- <u>Heaven</u>, by Joni Eareckson Tada
- <u>Shattered Dreams: God's Unexpected Pathway to Joy</u>, by Larry Crabb
- <u>When God Doesn't Make Sense</u>, by James Dobson
- <u>Through the Gates of Splendour</u>, by Elizabeth Elliot
- <u>The Mourning Book</u>, by Helen Fitzgerald
- <u>In the Unlikely Event of a Water Landing: a Geography of Grief</u>, by Christopher Noel
- <u>Starting Over- Help for Young Widows and Widowers</u>, by Adele Rice Nudel
- <u>Letters to my Husband</u>, by Fern Field Brooks
- <u>Being a Widow</u>, by Lynn Caine

- Don't Take my Grief Away, by Doug Manning
- Grief as a Family Process, Ester Shapiro
- I'm Grieving as Fast as I Can, by Linda Feinberg
- If God is so Good, why do I Hurt so Bad?, by David Biebel
- God Works the Night Shift, by Ron Mehl
- Living with Loss - Meditations for the Grieving, by Ellen Sue Stern
- The Complete Financial Guide for Single Parents, by Larry Burkett
- Early Widow, by Mary Jane Worden
- Someday Heaven, by Lary Libby
- When a Parent Dies, by Fred Bratman
- When Children Grieve, by John James
- Winter Holding Spring, by Crescent Dragonwagon
- Learning to Say Good-bye, by Eda LeShan
- Helping Children Cope with Separation and Loss, by Claudia L. Jewett
- It Must Hurt a Lot, by Doris Sanford
- Telling My Sister's Story, by Catherine Ripplinger Fenwick
- On Death and Dying, by Elizabeth Kubler-Ross
- Two-Part Invention, The Story of a Marriage, by Madeleine L'Engle
- Getting Through the Night, by Eugenia Price
- Mourning into Dancing, by Walter Wangerin
- Good Grief, by Granger Westburg
- Helping Children Grieve, by Theresa Huntley
- In the Arms of God, by James Dobson
- When God Weeps, by Joni Eareckson Tada and Steven Estes
- The Single Symphony- A Single Parent Grief Guide, by Suzy Yehl Marta
- A Time to Grieve: Meditation for Healing After the Death of a Loved One, by Carol Staudacher

- <u>Swallowed by a Snake: The Gift of the Masculine Side of Healing</u>, by Tom Golden
- <u>When a Man Faces Grief</u>, by Thomas Golden and James Miller
- <u>From My Grieving Heart to Yours</u>, by Dr. Charles Shepson
- <u>A Grace Disguised</u>, by Gerald L. Sittser
- <u>Life is Tough but God is Faithful</u>, by Sheila Walsh
- <u>Grief for a Season</u>, by Mildred Tengbom
- <u>The Mourning Handbook</u>, by Helen Fitzgerald
- <u>Blessed are those who Mourn</u>, (for Catholics) by Glenn Spencer
- <u>Facing Change (For Teens)</u> by Donna O'Toole, (Compassion Press) - available through New Hope
- <u>How I Feel</u>, (A Colouring Book for Children) by Alan Wolfelt - available through New Hope
- <u>Parenting With Wit and Wisdom in Times of Chaos and Loss</u>, by Barbara Coloroso
- <u>Life and Loss: A Guide to Help Grieving Children</u>, by Linda Goldman
- <u>Breaking the Silence: A Guide to Help Children with Complicated Grief/Suicide, Homicide, AIDS & Abuse</u>, by Linda Goldman
- <u>Tear Soup</u>, by Pat Schweibert, Chuck DeKlyen

Movies To Watch
- One True Thing
- Shadowlands
- Sarah, Plain and Tall (Great to Watch with kids of all ages)

LET'S HAVE SOME FUN!

Senior Moments

Three sisters ages 92, 94 and 96 live in a house together. One night the 96 year old draws a bath. She puts her foot in and pauses. She yells to the other sisters, "Was I getting in or out of the bath?"

The 94-year-old yells back, "I don't know. I'll come up and see." She starts up the stairs and pauses. "Was I going up the stairs or down?"

The 92 year old is sitting at the kitchen table having tea listening to her sisters. She shakes her head and says, "I sure hope I never get that forgetful," as she knocked on her wooden table for good measure. "She then yells, "I'll come up and help both of you as soon as I see who's at the door."

"I Can Hear Just Fine!"

Three retirees, each with a hearing loss, were playing golf one fine March day. One remarked to the other, "Windy, isn't it?" "No," the second man replied, "It's Thursday." And the third man chimed in, "So am I. Let's have a beer."

What A Choice

A little old lady was running up and down the halls in a nursing home. As she walked, she would flip up the hem of her nightgown and say, "Supersex." She walked up to an elderly man in a wheelchair. Flipping her gown at him, she said, "Supersex."

He sat silently for a moment or two and finally answered, "I'll take the soup."

Old Friends

Two elderly ladies had been friends for many decades. Over the years, they had shared all kinds of activities and adventures. Lately, their activities had been limited to meeting a few times a week to play cards. One day, they were playing cards when one looked at the other and said, "Now don't get mad at me. I know we've been friends for a long time, but I just can't think of your name! I've thought and thought, but I can't remember it. Please tell me what your name is." Her friend glared at her. For at least three minutes she just stared and glared at her. Finally she said, "How soon do you need to know?"

Senior Driving

As a senior citizen was driving down the highway, his cell phone rang. Answering, he heard his wife's voice urgently warning him, "Herman, I just heard on the news that there's a car going the wrong way on Interstate 77. Please be careful!" "Hell," said Herman, "It's not just one car. It's hundred's of them!"

Driving

Two elderly women were out driving in a large car. Both could barely see over the dashboard. As they were cruising along, they came to an intersection. The stoplight was red, but they just went on through. The woman in the passenger seat thought to herself "I must be losing it. I could have sworn we just went through a red light."

After a few more minutes, they came to another intersection and the light was red again.

Again, they went right through. The woman in the passenger seat was almost sure that the light had been red but was really concerned that she was losing it!

She was getting nervous. At the next intersection, sure enough, the light was red and they went on through. So, she turned to the other woman and said, "Mildred, do you know that we just ran through three red lights in a row? You could have killed us both!"

Mildred turned to her and said, "Crap, am I driving?"

9-1-1 Call

An elderly Floridian called 911 on her cell phone to report that her car has been broken into. She is hysterical as she explains her situation to the dispatcher: "They've stolen the stereo, the steering wheel, the brake pedal and even the accelerator!" she cried.

The dispatcher say, "Stay calm, Ma'am, an officer is on the way."

A few minutes later, the officer radios in.

"Disregard." He says. "She got in the back seat by mistake."

ORDER FORM

TRANSITION: *From Widowhood To Womanhood*

(A resource handbook for widows)

(NOTE: Prices listed below include 6% sales tax + S/H)

QTY	Description	Price	Total
	Transition Book	12.95	
	Transition Audio CD *(Tips Only)*	14.25	
	TOTAL ENCLOSED:		

Discounts available on 10 copies or more.
For more information contact us at
(313) 330-4490 or leavesofgold.llc@gmail.com

Name: _____

Phone: _____

Address: _____

City: _____State: _____ Zip: _____

Email: _____

Checks should be made payable to and Mail to:
Minister Mary Edwards
P.O. Box 21818 - Detroit, MI 48221 *or go to*
LeavesOfGoldConsulting.com to place your order online.

www.ingramcontent.com/pod-product-compliance
Lightning Source LLC
Chambersburg PA
CBHW072011060426
42446CB00042B/2298